T0049747

KETANJI

JUSTICE JACKSON'S JOURNEY TO THE U.S. SUPREME COURT

For all the Black girls who dare to dream.
—K.M.

For my parents, James and Trudy, who
encouraged me to follow my dreams.
—L.F.

Quill Tree Books is an imprint of HarperCollins Publishers.

Ketanji: Justice Jackson's Journey to the U.S. Supreme Court
Text copyright © 2023 by Kekla Magoon
Illustrations copyright © 2023 by Laura Freeman
All rights reserved. Printed in Italy.
No part of this book may be used or reproduced in any manner
whatsoever without written permission except in the case of
brief quotations embodied in critical articles and reviews. For
information address HarperCollins Children's Books, a division of
HarperCollins Publishers, 195 Broadway, New York, NY 10007.
www.harpercollins.com

Library of Congress Control Number: 2023930914
ISBN 978-0-06-329616-9

The artist used Photoshop to create the digital illustrations for this book.
Typography by Rachel Zegar
24 25 26 27 RTLO 10 9 8 7 6 5 4 3 2
First Edition

KETANJI

JUSTICE JACKSON'S JOURNEY TO THE U.S. SUPREME COURT

written by **Kekla Magoon**

illustrated by **Laura Freeman**

Quill Tree Books
An Imprint of HarperCollinsPublishers

Ketanji Onyika Brown was born to shine. Her parents wanted her to have a deep sense of heritage as well as a promise of her potential, so they gave her a name meaning "lovely one," a name with West African roots. They dreamed of great things for their beautiful child.

Ketanji's parents dressed her in West African clothing and kept her curly hair natural. They had been civil rights activists in the 1960s, and those years of struggling for equality and opportunity inspired them. They instilled in their daughter a belief that she could be and do anything she wanted, just by being herself.

From a young age, Ketanji knew she wanted to be a lawyer like her father. When he would pull out a big stack of legal books, Ketanji would pile up her coloring books alongside him and get to work.

Ketanji's special star twinkled every time she said her name. She often had to spell it for people who had never heard it before. Ketanji was proud of who she was, and proud of being different.

Sometimes being different made it hard to fit in, but she chose to ignore anyone who thought she didn't belong.

Her leadership skills came through more and more as she grew. She was elected mayor of Palmetto Junior High School and later became student body president of Miami Palmetto Senior High.

She joined the debate team, where she learned to write speeches, study opposing points of view, and prepare a logical argument.

Competing with the team gave her self-confidence and helped her build the courage to face big challenges.

Ketanji dazzled audiences and judges with her speaking style. She even won a national speech competition in her senior year.

Ketanji still dreamed of being a lawyer and, eventually, a judge. But despite all her achievements, some people struggled to see past the color of her skin. A guidance counselor discouraged her from applying to Harvard, one of the country's top colleges, saying it wasn't smart to aim too high.

I'll show her, Ketanji thought.

She knew that if you don't aim high, you'll never know what true heights you can reach. She refused to limit herself based on someone else's opinion. So Ketanji applied to Harvard, and not only did she get in, she quickly rose to the top of her class.

Ketanji still shined onstage. She performed improv theater with a troupe
of her college classmates. Improv is short for improvisation, which means

the actors don't have a script—they make up everything on the spot. She
enjoyed both the challenge and the applause for a job well done.

Ketanji always put her schoolwork first, but when social issues arose on campus, Ketanji stood up for justice. One time, her friends staged a protest when a fellow student hung a Confederate flag, which many people regarded as a symbol of racism, in his dorm room window.

Another time, they marched to protest the lack of Black teachers at Harvard. Ketanji supported the protests, but all the short-term problems her friends protested had roots in long-term problems like racism.

Ketanji wanted to fight for change in bigger ways too.

Ketanji's motto was "work first, play later," but she always kept her door open for friends to gather. Talking to diverse people was important to her. Debate team had taught her that hearing a range of opinions would help her better understand the world and support her in shaping her own views.

Ketanji's close friends and roommates were all very different, so they celebrated each other's gifts, learned from one another, and lifted each other up. Together, they became stronger.

A premed student named Patrick Jackson noticed Ketanji's shining light. Ketanji thought he was pretty special too. They were opposites in some ways but also shared core values of hard work, service, and treating people fairly.

The couple dated through college, then Ketanji attended
law school at Harvard while Patrick was in medical school.
Their lives became intertwined forever when they married
and had two daughters.

Ketanji still wished to become a judge someday, but first she had to practice as a lawyer. She hoped to find the perfect job—something exciting and challenging that would also allow her to juggle family, motherhood, and work. She was eager to find a new way to shine.

She started out as a law clerk, doing research to assist a judge. Next, she joined a private law firm in Washington, DC. She soon accepted a prestigious clerkship with U.S. Supreme Court Justice Stephen Breyer.

When she and her family moved to Boston, she joined a large firm, where the hours were long and the cases very stressful. She even worked as a public defender, a lawyer paid by the state to represent people who cannot afford a lawyer.

All in all, Ketanji held ten different jobs in a span of fifteen years. But none was quite right, and she feared her star had dimmed.

Ketanji became a federal judge in 2012 when President Obama nominated her for a position on the U.S. District Court. Her wide range of experience as a lawyer made her ideal for the role.

She understood many areas of law because she'd held so many different jobs. She enjoyed listening to cases and making legal decisions.

Finally Ketanji had found the right path—being a judge was the perfect job for her.

When there came an opening on the U.S. Supreme Court, Ketanji's daughter Leila wrote to President Obama about her mom.

Dear Mr. President,

While you are considering judges to fill Justice Scalia's seat on the Supreme Court, I would like to add my mother, Ketanji Brown Jackson of the District Court, to the list.

I, her daughter, Leila Jackson of 11 years old, strongly believe that she would be an excellent fit for the position. She is determined, honest, and never breaks a promise to anyone even if there are other things she'd rather do. She can demonstrate commitment, and is loyal, and never brags. I think she would make a great Supreme Court justice even if the workload will be larger on the court or if you have other nominees. Please consider her aspects for the job.

Thank you for listening,

Leila Jackson

Ketanji glowed with pride upon reading the note. Her daughter's words showed her she had succeeded at her goal of being a good lawyer and a good mother at the same time. She didn't have to be perfect at everything to be able to share her light.

Ketanji laughed quite a bit, too, at the thought that she could be a nominee to the nation's highest court. But her daughters had big dreams for their mother, and in her heart, Ketanji still believed in aiming high. There had never been a Black woman justice on the Supreme Court . . . someone had to be the first.

A few years later, President Joe Biden nominated Ketanji for a seat on the U.S. Court of Appeals. As a federal judge, confirmed by the Senate, she was in a prime position to be nominated to the Supreme Court for real.

Sure enough, just a year later, the call came. President Biden nominated Ketanji for a seat on the U.S. Supreme Court, thanks to her skills as a lawyer and her track record as a judge.

For four long days, Ketanji sat bravely before the Senate Judiciary Committee, with her daughters and husband looking on and people around the world watching too. She had faced Congress several times before, but this was the biggest job interview ever.

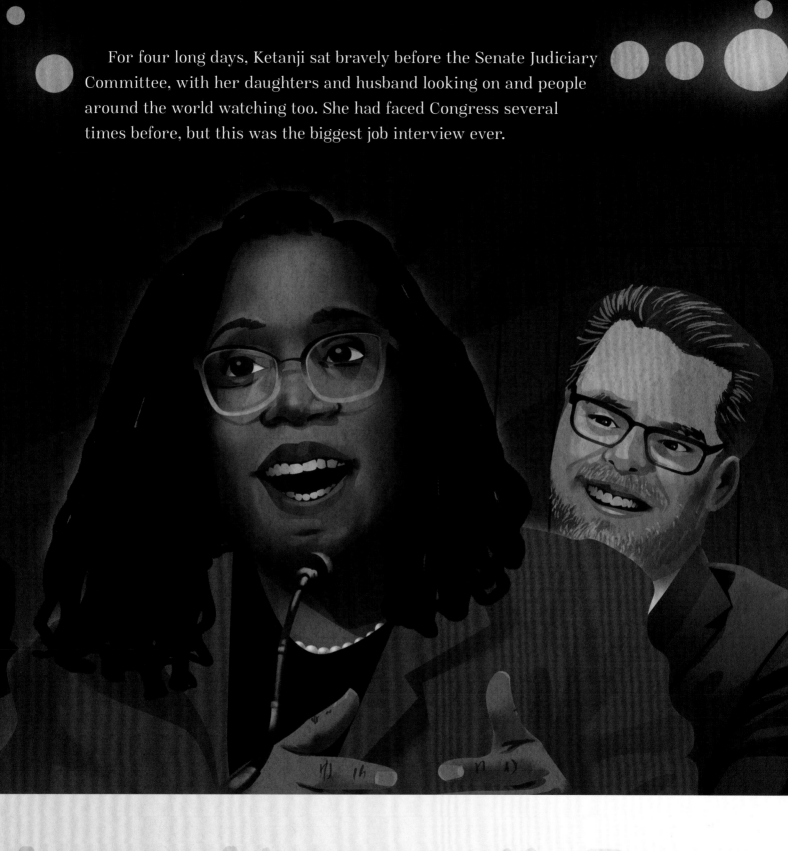

Hon. Ketanji Bro

Each senator on the committee had a turn to ask a few questions. Some senators used their time to support Ketanji, giving her a chance to speak about her experience and her values.

Others tried to criticize her or rile her up, but Ketanji stayed calm. Her voice never wavered as she looked each senator in the eye.

Ketanji's shining star beamed outward from that place. Several people in the room were brought to tears by her strength and determination. All around the country, people tuned in from their living rooms, on car radios, in classrooms, in their offices, on their phones, or from wherever they were to bear witness. The hopes and dreams of many Americans—young and old, Black and otherwise, lawyers and students and mothers and teachers and more—became tied up in Ketanji's story. The whole country held its breath, waiting to see if she could break a new barrier, something no one before her had done.

On April 7, 2022, the U.S. Senate voted to confirm her nomination. Ketanji Brown Jackson would become the first Black woman on the U.S. Supreme Court. She well remembered being a small girl wearing Afro puffs and a dashiki, announcing her name proudly and setting her sights high.

When she accepted the confirmation, she said, "It has taken two hundred and thirty-two years . . . but we've made it." She added, "Our children are telling me that they see now, more than ever, that here in America, anything is possible."

Today, Justice Ketanji Brown Jackson's star shines as brightly as ever, and now the whole world can see her light.

AUTHOR'S NOTE

Ketanji Onyika Brown was born on September 14, 1970, in Washington, DC. Her parents, Johnny and Ellery Brown, were former sharecroppers and civil rights activists. When Ketanji was four, her family moved to Miami so that her father could attend law school. Ketanji's earliest memories are of watching her father study and working alongside him.

Ketanji describes her childhood as "terrific but normal." She served on student council in middle school and high school and joined the debate team, where she excelled. She won the National Catholic Forensic League championship her senior year.

Ketanji graduated magna cum laude from Harvard, which meant she was in the top one percent of her class. She went on to Harvard Law School, where she served as supervising editor of the Harvard Law Review (a prestigious writing and editing position) and graduated cum laude, which meant she was in the top ten percent of her class.

Ketanji married Dr. Patrick Jackson in 1996. Their divergent upbringings—she the daughter of Black sharecroppers and he a white Bostonian who could trace his lineage back to England before the *Mayflower*—did not prevent them from finding comfort and common ground in one another. They have two daughters, Talia and Leila.

Leila's letter to President Obama was probably not the main thing that put Judge Jackson on the short list for the Supreme Court—her judicial record would have taken care of that in time—but it is still a great example of a young person being strong and speaking up, sharing their opinion with a person in power. It is not always easy to speak up about the things that are most important to us, but telling elected officials what we think is best for our country is an important part of citizenship, no matter how old or young we are.

Beyond her race and gender, Ketanji's wide experience as a lawyer and judge makes her a unique voice on the court. She is the first Supreme Court justice ever who has past experience as a public defender, and she is one of few current justices who attended public school. She has worked for large and small firms, for the government, and as a clerk within the judiciary and even served on the Sentencing Commission, which helps create guidelines that judges all over the country must follow.

In her acceptance speech after her judicial confirmation, Ketanji paid tribute to her parents and grandparents as well as the many trailblazing women and Black leaders who paved the way for her to have this opportunity. "I am just the very lucky first inheritor of the dream of liberty and justice for all," she said. "No one does this on their own." She also spoke of the challenge and responsibility of being a role model for the young people watching from around the country and around the world. The letters she received from children reminded her of the hope and potential inherent in us all.

Ketanji Brown Jackson was sworn in as associate justice of the United States Supreme Court on June 30, 2022. May her light continue to shine from the bench for many years to come.

GLOSSARY

Confederate flag — Also called the "Stars and Bars" or the "Southern Cross," this flag represented the states that seceded from the Union during the Civil War to form the Confederate States of America. Flying the flag today is a controversial act because it is a historical reminder of a time when Black people were enslaved.

Dashiki — A West African style of shirt, often cut from bright patterned fabric with an elaborate embroidered collar.

Improv — Short for "improvisational." It refers to a type of theater performance in which actors make up their actions and dialogue on the spot instead of performing from a script.

Judge — A public official authorized to decide upon questions brought before a court. Judges are either elected or appointed, depending on where they practice. Federal judges are appointed by the president.

Judicial confirmation — When Congress votes on a judicial nominee, deciding whether to accept the president's recommended choice and let them become a judge.

Judicial nomination — When a person's name is put forward for consideration to become a judge. Federal judges (like Supreme Court justices) are nominated by the president and submitted to Congress for confirmation.

Law clerk — A person who supports a judge (or another lawyer) by helping with research, writing, and legal analysis.

Law firm — A group of lawyers who work together in business. Law firms can be small, with two or three lawyers, midsized, with a dozen or more lawyers, or large, with hundreds of lawyers.

Law review — A journal run by law students that publishes articles by legal professionals like lawyers and judges as well as shorter pieces called "notes" or "comments" written by law students. Being selected to serve on your school's law review is a prestigious opportunity.

Lawyer — A person who provides legal advice and counsel to others and represents them in court. A person becomes a lawyer by earning a juris doctor degree in law school and passing one or more state bar exams to receive a license to practice.

Private law firm — When a lawyer runs their own business representing their choice of clients rather than working for the government or representing a single company.

Public defender — A lawyer employed by the government whose job is to represent people who cannot afford legal representation.

Senate Judiciary Committee — The group of senators assigned to make decisions about federal judges and federal court.

U.S. District Court — There are ninety-four district courts around the country, with at least one in each state and the District of Columbia. Their role is to resolve disputes by studying the facts of each case and applying legal principles to decide who is right.

U.S. Sentencing Commission — A bipartisan agency that develops federal sentencing policy. It decides what punishment fits each type of crime that a person can be convicted of under U.S. federal law and publishes documents that help judges around the country deliver fair and consistent rulings.

U.S. Supreme Court — The highest court in the United States, whose nine justices make rulings that affect federal law throughout the country.

TIMELINE

September 14, 1970: Ketanji Onyika Brown born in Washington, DC

1988: Ketanji graduates from Miami Palmetto Senior High School, where she was senior class president and speech/debate team champion

1992: Ketanji graduates magna cum laude from Harvard University

1992–93: Ketanji works as a reporter for *Time* magazine

1996: Ketanji graduates cum laude from Harvard Law School, where she served as supervising editor of the Harvard Law Review in her final year

1996: Ketanji marries Patrick Jackson, taking his last name

1996: Ketanji clerks for Massachusetts District Court Judge Patti B. Saris

1997: Ketanji clerks for Judge Bruce M. Selya of the U.S. Court of Appeals for the First Circuit

1998: Ketanji works for private firm in DC, Miller Cassidy Larroca & Lewin

1999: Ketanji clerks for Associate Justice Stephen G. Breyer of the U.S. Supreme Court

2000: Ketanji works for private firm in Boston, Goodwin Procter

2000: Ketanji and Patrick's first daughter, Talia, is born

2002: Ketanji works for DC firm, Feinberg and Rozen

2003: Ketanji joins the U.S. Sentencing Commission as assistant special counsel

2004: Ketanji and Patrick's second daughter, Leila, is born

2005: Ketanji serves as a federal public defender in DC

2007: Ketanji works for DC firm, Morrison & Foerster

July 23, 2009: President Obama nominates Ketanji as vice chair of the U.S. Sentencing Commission, leading to her first appearance before the Senate Judiciary Committee

February 11, 2010: The Senate confirms Ketanji for this role

September 20, 2012: President Obama nominates Ketanji as a district court judge for the U.S. Circuit Court, leading to her second appearance before the Senate Judiciary Committee

March 22, 2013: The Senate confirms Ketanji for this role

2016: Ketanji joins the Board of Overseers at Harvard University for a six-year term

March 30, 2021: President Biden nominates Ketanji to serve on the U.S. Court of Appeals for the DC Circuit, leading to her third appearance before the Senate Judiciary Committee

June 14, 2021: Ketanji begins serving on the U.S. Court of Appeals

February 25, 2022: President Biden nominates Ketanji to replace Justice Breyer, who plans to retire from the U.S. Supreme Court

March 2022: Senate confirmation hearings

April 7, 2022: The Senate confirms Ketanji for this role, in a 53-47 vote

June 30, 2022: Ketanji Brown Jackson is sworn in as the newest associate justice of the U.S. Supreme Court by Chief Justice John Roberts, who administered the constitutional oath, and the retiring Justice Breyer, who administered the judicial oath

BIBLIOGRAPHY

"35th Edith House Lecture: Ketanji Brown Jackson, U.S. District Court for the District of Columbia." YouTube, March 23, 2017.

Blanco, Adrian, and Shelly Tan. "How Ketanji Brown Jackson's Path to the Supreme Court Differs from the Current Justices." The *Washington Post*, WP Company, March 20, 2022. www.washingtonpost.com/politics/interactive/2022/ketanji-brown -jackson-school-career

Fabio, Michelle. "What Is a Law Review and How Is It Important?" ThoughtCo, February 21, 2019. www.thoughtco.com/what-is -law-review-2154872

Fisher, Marc, Ann E. Marimow, and Lori Rozsa. "How Ketanji Brown Jackson Found a Path between Confrontation and Compromise." The *Washington Post*, WP Company, February 26, 2022. www.washingtonpost.com/politics/2022/02/25 /ketanji-brown-jackson-miami-family-parents

"Judge Ketanji Brown Jackson." United States Senate Committee on the Judiciary. Accessed June 21, 2022. www.judiciary.senate .gov/judge-ketanji-brown-jackson

"Ketanji Brown Jackson to Serve on the U.S. Supreme Court." The White House, the United States Government, April 7, 2022. www.whitehouse.gov/kbj

"Ketanji Brown Jackson: Legal Career Timeline." Southern Poverty Law Center, April 7, 2022. www.splcenter.org /news/2022/04/07/ketanji-brown-jackson-legal-career-timeline

Lewis, Nicole. "Ketanji Brown Jackson and the Politics of Black Hair." *Slate* magazine, April 7, 2022. slate.com/news-and -politics/2022/04/ketanji-brown-jacksons-hair-is-historic.html

McDaniel, Eric. "Jackson Notes the Progress She Represents in Her Journey to the Supreme Court." NPR, April 8, 2022. www .npr.org/2022/04/08/1091459152/biden-harris-jackson-senate-historic-confirmation-vote

Merriam-Webster.com

PBSNewsHour. "Watch Live: Judge Ketanji Brown Jackson Sworn in as First Black Woman on Supreme Court." PBSNewsHour, June 30, 2022. www.pbs.org/newshour/politics/watch-live-judge-ketanji-brown-jackson-sworn-in-as-first-black-woman -on-supreme-court

———. "Watch: Judge Ketanji Brown Jackson's Opening Statement in Supreme Court Confirmation Hearings." PBSNewsHour, March 21, 2022. www.pbs.org/newshour/politics/watch-judge-ketanji-brown-jackson-pledges-to-decide-cases-without -fear-or-favor-in-hearing-opening-statement

U.S. Court of Appeals — D.C. Circuit — Ketanji Brown Jackson. Accessed June 21, 2022. www.cadc.uscourts.gov/internet/home .nsf/Content/VL+-+Judges+-+KBJ

"Video: Ketanji Brown Jackson's Full Speech after Historic Supreme Court Confirmation — CNN Video." Cable News Network, April 8, 2022. www.cnn.com/videos/politics/2022/04/08/ketanji-brown-jackson-supreme-court-celebration-full-speech -sot-vpx.cnn

FURTHER READING

Highest Tribute: Thurgood Marshall's Life, Leadership, and Legacy, The by Kekla Magoon, illustrated by Laura Freeman, Quill Tree Books, New York, 2021.

Turning Pages: My Life Story by Sonia Sotomayor, illustrated by Lulu Delacre, Philomel Books, New York, 2018.

I Dissent: Ruth Bader Ginsburg Makes Her Mark by Debbie Levy, illustrated by Elizabeth Baddeley, Simon & Schuster, New York, 2016.

Kamala Harris: Rooted in Justice by Nikki Grimes, illustrated by Laura Freeman, Atheneum, New York, 2020.

Hidden Figures: The True Story of Four Black Women and the Space Race by Margot Lee Shetterly, illustrated by Laura Freeman, Harper, New York, 2018.

Not Done Yet: Shirley Chisholm's Fight for Change by Tameka Fryer Brown, illustrated by Nina Crews, Millbrook Press, Minneapolis, 2022.

"And Still I Rise" by Maya Angelou, poem, 1978.